SURRENDER TO THE SILENCE

*To Judy —
Teacher extraordinaire
May God bless you
today & always,
Sharon*

SURRENDER TO THE SILENCE

SHARON DEXTER

eLectio Publishing
Little Elm, Texas
www.eLectioPublishing.com

Surrender to the Silence
By Sharon Dexter
Copyright © 2013 by Sharon Dexter. All rights reserved
Cover copyright © 2013 by eLectio Publishing. All rights reserved.
ISBN: 0615924417
ISBN-13: 978-0615924410

All poems contained in this work are previously unpublished, exclusive of the following works:
"Growth … Sin: Personally" appeared in *Purpose* (2007)
"Growth … Changed: Use Me" appeared in *Devo'Zine* (2004)
"Jesus … His Victory: Easter Miracle" appeared in *Partners* (2004)
"My Response … Actions: My Friend, I Hold You" appeared in *Devo'Zine* (2011)

Unless otherwise noted, Scripture taken from *The Message*. Copyright © 1993, 1994, 1995, 1996, 2000, 2001, 2002. Used by permission of NavPress Publishing Group.

Scriptures marked "NASB" taken from the NEW AMERICAN STANDARD BIBLE®, Copyright © 1960, 1962, 1963, 1968, 1971, 1972, 1973, 1975, 1977, 1995 by The Lockman Foundation. Used by permission.

Surrender to the Silence

Surrender to the silence.
Listen to the pulse of wonder.
Diffuse the shadows of the darkness.
Life is more than merely living.

Contents

Faith ... Begin

    As a Young Child   1

    Early Morning   2

    The Church   3

    Attention   4

    Stones will Cry (Haiku)   5

    Do I?   6

    Discipleship   7

Faith ... Grow ... Pray

    Learning   8

    Inconstant   9

    May We Have   10

    Echo of The Prayer   11

    Get Behind Me!   12

    Before They Call   13

    Lord, I Pray   14

    In Thy Name   15

Faith ... Grow ... Worship

    Distractions   16

    Sensing the Lord   17

    A Psalm for Simplicity   18

Faith ... Grow ... Bible

    Wrapped in the Word   19

    Journaling   21

    Nuggets   22

Faith ... Grow ... Serve

    Lord, I'm Coming   23

    By These Things   24

Faith … Grow … Faith in the Process

    Rocks and Briars   25

    Family Values   26

    Eyes   27

    Attractions   28

    Help Me Understand   29

    I / You   30

    The Frame   31

    Be Still   32

    Genuine   33

    While   34

Growth … Sin

    A Lousy Housekeeper   35

    Direction   36

    Personally   37

    That Thought   38

    Come Near   39

    Promise   40

    Crossroads   41

Growth … Repent

    Hear My Plea   43

    My Dirt   44

    This is My Song   45

    With   46

    By Your Mercies   47

    In the Valley   48

    Revive My Heart   49

Growth … Forgiven

    The Music of Hell   50

Enough	51
Cleansed	52
Again … and Again	53

Growth … Changed

Your Sheep	54
Maturing	55
Blessed Are They	56
I Was Walking	57
Mundane	58
That Bump	59
Pruned	60
Strengthen Your Core	61
The Ninety and Nine	62
Chaff	63
Use Me	64
In the shadow	65
Selah!	66

Growth … Obey

Because	67
Prone to Wallow	68
Generosity	69
I Choose You	70
If We Refuse	71
Lord, You Called Me	73

God's Attributes … Creator

In His Hand	74
Soul-ful	75
Winter White	76
I Behold	77

Patchwork Quilt	78
You Created My Soul	79
God's Attributes … Protector	
My Rock	80
Shout!	81
The Secret Place	82
Lost or Found	83
God of Storms	84
Psalm on God's Majesty	85
God's Attributes … Comforter	
Vacation Spot	86
The Joy of Rainbows	87
My Special Friend	88
Lord, You Were There	89
God's Quilt	90
Hush, Hush	91
God's Attributes … Promise-Keeper	
Thou Art the Lord	92
Proof?	93
A Good Thing	94
Your Song of Peace	95
God's Silence	96
Aging Process	97
I Do Not Know	98
How Could I Think?	99
Because of Your Love	100
Your Forever Love	101
God's Attributes … Forgiver	
The Patience of God	102

As Is	103
Behold	104
It's Impossible!	105
From the Dark	106
O Love of God	107
My Testimony	108
In Your Presence	109

God's Attributes … Awesome! You are GOD!

Song of Your Presence	110
Kingdom Eternity	111
Competition?	112
Not Competition	113
The Maze	114
I, the Lord	115
In My Deep-Dark	116
Springs	117
Geography of Life	118
Waters of Blessings	119
You Know Me!	120
Why Do You Care?	121
The Hiding Place of Thunder	122
Praise!	123
Beyond	125
My Distress	126
God of My Yesterday	127

Jesus … His Life

Heroes	128
The Visible Image	129
Joseph, the Forgotten Man	130

In This Season of Lent	131
Jesus … His Passion	
Fragrant Aroma?	132
Seder	133
Even Judas	134
Jesus, My Son	135
He Was	137
You Could Have	138
Jesus … His Victory	
Your World Is Glorious	139
Resurrection	140
Easter	141
Easter Miracle	142
A Question	143
Road to Emmaus	144
My Response … Attitudes	
Are You A Pharisee??	145
You Are	146
Just An Opinion?	147
My Attitude	148
Without Gratitude	149
My Joy	150
Destination Disease	151
How Could They?	152
The Goal	153
In My Silence	154
Be	155
I Will Not Be Silent	156
Flowing Love	157

My Song	158
Details	159
From the Bottom	160
Heart and Soul	161
A Psalm of Gratitude	162
Funeral Blessings	163

My Response … Actions

I Want to Be	164
Shoulda, Woulda, Coulda	165
Just Beyond Awareness	166
Heartbeat	167
It's My Choice	168
A Psalm for Fasting	169
Salt	170
But, Wait ….	171
God's Prism	172
Water From the Rock	173
Reconciliation	174
In Faith, Hope, and Love	175
Thy Light	176
You Are Who I Need	177
Bearing Your Burdens	178
My Friend, I Hold You	179
Commission	180
Engage the World	181

Faith ... Begin

As a Young Child

As a young child, I held onto my father's hand,
Crossing the busy thoroughfare.
Now I reach out, and put my life in Your hands,
Trusting that You will lead me home.

Faith ... Begin

Early Morning

Awake and sitting
On edge of my sleep-warmed bed
Contemplating Thee.

Wrapped in Love's blanket
Steeped in Thy merciful peace
How may I serve Thee?

Faith ... Begin

The Church
"The church, you see, is not peripheral to the world; the world is peripheral to the church." (Eph 1:22)

Which do we look to
For guidance or solace,
The church, or the world all around?
If world is our master
We're led to disaster;
The world is but honoring "self."

Thus looking to "church"
Is following God,
For Jesus, the Christ, is supreme.
"Church" would serve better
Than world 'ere attempted,
In actions, in word, and in love.

Faith ... Begin

Attention

I want to be
      At the edge of God's attention.
If I had His full attention,
      I'd be toast!

I need to pause;
      Give my God my full attention.
If I gave Him only the edge,
      I'd be lost!

Faith … Begin

Stones will Cry (Haiku)

Let the silence breathe,
Seep deep into conscious thought,
Or stones will cry out.

Faith ... Begin

Do I?

Do I hear You?
Do I listen?
        Not "IF" You call, but "When"?
Do I love You?
Really love You?
        And follow You through life?

Do I promise, Lord,
And ever strive
        To disregard my will?
Do I commit
To honor You
        And bow before Your way?

Faith … Begin

Discipleship

Disciples pray daily.
Well, guess I can try.
Surprised, I discover Christ, waiting for me.

Worshipping weekly:
The hymns, prayers, and sermons
His presence within me enlightens and comforts.

"Study the Bible."
In reading, I find
His guidance for life, and blessings on blessings!

Serve church, and serve others.
Responding to mercy
We find we've no option; discover we're *needed*.

Form Spiritual friendships.
Accountability
Holds one another responsible to God.

Encourage each other
Along the pathway
To closer communion with Jesus, our Savior.

Give Time, Talents, Treasure.
Time to be caring.
Tithing our treasures, talents empower.

In requesting I change,
He asked for too little,
For growing in faith enriches my life!

Faith ... Grow ... Pray

Learning

Learning to love Thee,
O Lord, I pray
For grace to creep closer
Day after day.
Week after week, Lord,
And year after year,
Help me stand close enough
To finally hear,
"Well-done, my good and faithful servant."

Faith ... Grow ... Pray

Inconstant

Inconstant
Or
Incompatible?
Pray unceasingly
But
Don't babble!

Faith ... Grow ... Pray

May We Have

Lord, may we have
Clear eyes to see
Sharp ears to hear
Minds to perceive
Wills to obey.

Faith … Grow … Pray

Echo of The Prayer

"Our Father,"
        The congregation, standing, intones
"Who art in heaven,"
        Wait … Do you hear them?
"Hallowed be Thy name."
        The echoes, in the background?
"Thy kingdom come,"
        Is that an echo from the catacombs?
"Thy will be done,
On earth as it is in heaven."
        Do you hear them?
        Simon Peter's baritone? Timothy's young tenor?
"Give us this day our daily bread."
        There .. another.
        I know I heard my father's voice.
"And forgive us our trespasses,
As we forgive those who trespass against us."
        And my sister, who died but a short year ago.
"Lead us not into temptation."
        Voices mingle, blend, rise
"But deliver us from evil."
        Together, past and present, we crescendo:
"For THINE is the kingdom,

And the power,
And the glory … FOREVER!"

        Silence speaks.
        Then, breathlessly, we whisper,
"Amen."

Faith ... Grow ... Pray

Get Behind Me!

Get behind me, Satan,
      Don't be rude!
I'm in another conversation
      With my God!

Get behind me, Satan,
      Go away!
I'm telling God how much I love Him.
      I'm in prayer!

Stop trying to distract me
      When I pray!
My God deserves my rapt attention
      Always!

Faith … Grow … Pray

Before They Call
(Isaiah 55:24)

I had not yet called out to You,
    But I felt Your Presence
    Calling out to me.
My mind was forming the question
    As the Spirit whispered
    What was in my heart.
I spoke the words of fear,
    Of worries, hope, despair,
    With overflowing tears.
Still praying, I was calmed.

Faith … Grow … Pray

Lord, I Pray

In my silence, Lord, I pray,
Strength to keep me day by day.
Aging bones that creak and moan
Mean they're waiting to go home.

Heaven's gates will open wide
As I rush to gain Your side.
Father, mother, sister too
Patiently stand next to you.

What a party that will be
Reuniting lord, with Thee
Gratefully, I've won my race
When I greet Thee, face to face!

Faith … Grow … Pray

In Thy Name

In Thy name, and for Thy sake,
Guide me on which path I take.
Keep my motivation clear.
Help me know there's naught to fear.
Purify my heart, O Lord,
As I meditate Thy Word.

Thank You for these words I pray.
May they NOT be merely words to say!

Faith ... Grow ... Worship

Distractions

My mind is a jumble, O Lord.
I do not worship as I ought.
A buzzing fly pulls my mind away.
A tickle in the throat requires attention.
I need a pillow behind my back.
Oh! I've a cramp in my big toe!
A chill down the spine,
The laughter of children outside…
Distractions, Lord,
Distractions have come between us.

Free my mind, Lord.
Help me concentrate, deeply,
      On you alone.
May my entire being
      Be open only to your presence.
Fill me with your glory, Lord
Let nothing else penetrate
      My absolute consciousness
      Of you.

Then will I worship truly, Lord.
My song rising like incense.
May the aroma of my love please you.
May I be faithful
      To my ever-faithful King!

Faith ... Grow ... Worship

Sensing the Lord

May I smell the aroma of blessings, O Lord,
As I taste sweet forgiveness of sin.
When I see all Your works,
I know my Creator
Will grant a new life to begin.

May I feel Your sweet loving surround me, O Lord,
As I hear You above the world's din.
Because of the Cross,
I know my Dear Savior
Sent Spirit to dwell deep within.

May I taste honeyed words from the Bible, O God,
As Your Word I peruse every day.
When I read my devotions,
And pray to the Father,
He guides me, and brightens my way.

May I hear the sweet sounds of the choir, O God,
As their voices in harmony raise.
May I lift up my voice
To join in the chorus,
As I sing of my thanks and my praise.

Faith ... Grow ... Worship

A Psalm for Simplicity

Gimme, Gimme, Gimme!!
That's the theme song of the nations, Lord.
MORE! Never enough!

I have, at times, joined that chorus.
But, spending time with You
       Teaches me of true need.
I need You! --- Only You!

Simplify the desires of my heart,
Douse the fires of earthly appetites.
Let me hunger for You, Lord.
MORE! Never enough!

Faith … Grow … Bible

Wrapped in the Word

A̲sk, it will be given you
B̲e kind to one another
C̲ome, all burdened
D̲o good to all
E̲levate the downtrodden.

F̲ollow Him
G̲o, and tell
H̲e has risen!
I̲saiah foretold-
J̲esus rules!
SO…

K̲nock at the door, and it will be opened.
L̲ove all your enemies.
M̲any are called.
N̲ot all will obey.
O̲h, ye of little faith!

P̲ray, ye. without ceasing, as He
Q̲uiets rushing waters.
R̲estoring the soul,
S̲oft words turn wrath away.
T̲eacher, show Your miracles.

U̲nderstand, then turn, to heal your soul.
V̲erily, open your ears.
W̲idows and orphans, be comforted
E̲xtra tunic, don't bring.
Y̲ou shall teach, and preach.
Z̲echariah's son, John, has proclaimed Him!

Follow Him

Go, and tell
He has risen!
Isaiah foretold-
Jesus rules!

All Hail to the KING! All Hail!

Faith ... Grow ... Bible

Journaling

We talk, Lord,
And I ponder Your words.
As I listen to You, I find my hand writing
Nuggets of understanding,
      Or thoughts
      Or questions
      To go over again.

In my solitude
      Our discussions within my mind
      Often flow as babbling brooks
          Over stony distractions.
Sometimes the river of thought
      Gently proceeds toward Your destination.
If I failed to write,
I would fail to remember.

I have learned, Lord,
      The more honest,
      The more open,
      The more transparent my writing becomes,
The warmer Your smile,
      The clearer Your words,
      The deeper my love.

Yesterday, I wrote,
      "Lord, I see it!
      I see Your unfailing love!"
Today I begin with praise.
You are the God of life!
This I will never forget,
      But I will write it again.
          And again.

Faith ... Grow ... Bible

Nuggets

There are mornings when I
Can't stop the perusal
At "designated" endings
Of devotional readings.
If I stopped, I would miss
Such magnificent nuggets
As "spare me so I
Can smile once again,
'fore I'm gone, and I cease
To exist." and, "Let all
Who seek You rejoice."

Your Word *always* blesses

Faith … Grow … Serve

Lord, I'm Coming

Lord, I'm coming! Help me listen.
Help me give my life to Thee.
Help me always heed my Savior.
Help me live my life for Thee.
Come, I'll worship.
Thee I worship!
Let me give my ALL for Thee!

Lord, I linger, at your feet
As You speak Your word to me.
As You train me to deliver
Love, and mercies, blessings free---
All to others,
Sisters, Brothers,
All united, Lord, in Thee.

Faith ... Grow ... Serve

By These Things

As a Christian, Lord, I love you.
By these things, they'll know it's true.
I will praise Your name, O Lord!
Forever, and forever!

I promise I will daily pray,
Have conversations with my Lord.
I'll commit to worship weekly,
Adoring Father, Son, and Spirit …
Adoring Spirit, Father, Son.
To read my Bible every day
Will be my great delight, my Lord.
I will also find it joyous
To serve You here, as well as elsewhere.
To serve You every way I can.

Lord, with Your Spirit, I will try
To form a friendship strong and true.
Then, together, we'll attempt to
Encourage friends to grow beside us.
Encourage other friends to grow.
Lord, I commit to give my time,
My talents, and my treasure too.
Giving You of time, of talents,
And treasure will but bless me fully.
Yes, I will give my all for You.

As a Christian, Lord, I love you.
By these things, they'll know it's true.
I will praise Your name, O Lord!
Forever, and forever!

Faith … Grow … Faith in the Process

Rocks and Briars

I can't seem to get out of bed;
I'm tired all the time.
My darn head is aching again.
My back is a total mess.
I woke to hear my breathing squeak,
And I'm still breathing heavy.

BUT
Sleep before midnight is better,
So being tired is all my own fault!
Though it aches, my head isn't roaring.
Sitting quietly relieves my back pain;
And breathing has eased as well.

Sitting here, in the Presence of God,
I realize you have placed my life
Along pleasant paths.
I humbly thank you!
Out of the abundance of blessings,
May I help others
Whose pathway has more
Rocks and briars.

Faith … Grow … Faith in the Process

Family Values

We teach our children how to live
By how we react in our world.

Hate is not a family value,
Nor is prejudice,
Nor back fence gossiping, or our lies.

We pray our children will learn to act
According to Your Word
Anyway!

Faith ... Grow ... Faith in the Process

Eyes

Perspective on what
Is best, in God's eyes,
Can only be seen
Through the eyes of faith.

Believing in God,
Giving all to Him
Throws light on your path;
Convicts you of truth.
Keep your eyes on Him,
Be guided by Christ.
His way will be yours....
And blessed your path.

Faith ... Grow ... Faith in the Process

Attractions

The alluring shades of evil,
The distractions and attractions,
The sparkling lure of wicked ways ...
All, the devil's tools of death.
They strip the soul of inner strength,
They rip the calm, and love of life,
Destroy, and overcome our faith.
Then, the devil laughs at God.

The Lord provides His glorious light.
Like moths, attracted to the flame,
May we confess our darkest sin,
Repent, and ask for mercy.
He'll bless the soul with inner strength,
Supply serenity, and grace,
Restore, and bring our balance back.
Then, the Lord will laugh at death.

Faith … Grow … Faith in the Process

Help Me Understand
(Isaiah 6:9-10)

O Lord,
    Clear the scales from my eyes
        And let me see
    Unstop my ears
        That I may hear.
    Melt my hard heart
        And help me understand
Then, O Lord,
    Bid me come
        For healing.

Faith ... Grow ... Faith in the Process

I / You

I wonder, and You clarify;
I sin, and then You save.
I wander, and You rescue me,
I call, and listen. You respond.

May I love because You love me,
And act upon Your word.
May I accept Your guiding grace
As I go forth into Your world.

Faith … Grow … Faith in the Process

The Frame

Now I see in the mirror,
      Though dimly.
At times the mirror seems turned.
I strive to see Your image
      From the frame.

WAIT!!

<u>You</u> are the Frame
Through which I am given
      Whatever view You wish me to see
      At any given moment!

I look into the Frame,
To see myself
      As You see me.
Through Your reflection
      I now understand …
I am Your CHILD!

Faith ... Grow ... Faith in the Process

Be Still

Be still before the Lord.
Listen for His still, small voice.
How can you hear him
Through babbling in your mind?
Hush. Hush. Be still.

Now bask within His sight.
Bathe in radiant beams of love,
Clothe self in mercy.
Be still, and let Him speak.
Hold fast to Him!

Be still.
Be still before the Lord.

Faith ... Grow ... Faith in the Process

Genuine

Is my faith genuine?
In wilderness times,
      I wonder.

In crucible-testing,
My faith purified,
      Now strengthened.

Your love, everlasting,
Forestalls any doubt
      You are here!

My faith IS genuine!
Your Presence resides
      Deep within.

Faith ... Grow ... Faith in the Process

While

I cannot worry
While I am singing
     My songs
          Of praise
              To You!
I'm unable to worry
While truly trusting
     That You
          Control
              My soul.

God of the universe
God of creation
Manager of all that I see:
     How can I but love You?
     How can I but trust You?
     How can I but pray
         You will
             Take care of me?

Growth ... Sin

A Lousy Housekeeper

I'm a lousy housekeeper;
      Dust abounds.
He doesn't seem to notice the dirt ...
Ahh ... He does not <u>comment</u> about ...
Yea, He does!
      His WORD tells me:
           He sees
           He forgives
           He cleanses.
My soul glows with cleanliness ...
      Until the dust settles once again.

Growth ... Sin

Direction

Wrap my mind
Around the "I Believe!"

Loose the bonds
That tie me to "I want!"

Dissolve the stubborn streak
That shouts, "Oh, YES I CAN!!"

Push me toward the pathway
That tells me, "No, no, my child."

Freedom lies just beyond
The "Thou Shalt Not…"

All the way to Jesus,
Who bids me, "Come."

Growth ... Sin

Personally

I failed and neglected
      A promise I'd made,
      And scoffed, "Don't take it so seriously."
Your promise was kept,
      Your loss was my gain.
      You died, and You meant it personally.

            Hanging on Calvary
            You did it for me.
            I take it personally.

Growth ... Sin

That Thought
"Take delight in the Lord, and He will give you your heart's desire."
(Psalm 37:4)

My heart's desire
    Is deeply wanting You
    First in my life.
That thought
    Brings a smile
    To my soul!

If that desire
    Is deep within my heart,
    How will I change?
That thought
    Rolls an ice cube
    Down my life.

Resisting change,
    My demons fight with me.
    Evil? Or Good?
That thought
    Brings a lamp
    To my sin.

Jesus, my Lord,
    Is gently calling me:
    "Open your heart."
That thought
    Shows His love
    Completes me.

Growth ... Sin

Come Near
(James 4:8a)

I drifted, Lord.
The eddies of the world
      Pulled me away
      From safe haven
      Of Your Word.

Then troubles came.
The ebb tide of my sin
      Kept me away
      From Your Purpose
      For my life.

Your absence then
Was noted deep within,
      Called me to turn
      Back to Jesus
      Once again.

Returning to God,
I heard Your Voice once more
      Welcome me home
      From sin's clutches.
      I am safe.

Growth ... Sin

Promise

I promise, Lord.
      It's not the first time,
      For I often fall away.
My strength is You, Lord.
      This time, I ask for help
      To keep me on track.

When temptations rise, Lord,
      And they will, of course,
      Your WORD will shield me.
When You were tempted, Lord,
      You resisted Satan's cunning
      By quoting from the WORD.

So, Your example, Lord,
      Leads me to prepare
      By spending time with You.
I promise, Lord.
      Make this the last time!
      Keep me from failing again.

Growth ... Sin

Crossroads
(Proverbs 8: 1-4)

I am at a crossroad of life, Lord.
The pathway left, or right alike,
      Looks rather interesting.
Bright lights invite me forth,
Sounds of laughter enthrall.
      Just a short visit?
      What could it hurt?
I am sorely tempted.

Wisdom stands at the crossroad,
Pointing straight ahead.
Spoilsport!
Where's the fun down that narrow lane?
But ... I remember wandering
      Down one intriguing lane.
Found people, ignorant of His Word,
      Urging me to do evil ..
      Both in God's sight and in my own.
Each time I've walked off on my own,
      I stumbled.

This time…
Wisdom opens The Book … and reads …
      And nods again toward the straight path.
I strain to hear the slight strand of sound.
The more I listen, the more distractions fade.
Finally, I hear,
      "Hallelujah! Worthy is the Lamb!"
I know that song!
I smile.
<u>This</u> time,
 I will listen to Wisdom.

Temptation averted,
> I am granted
>> A view of His Glory!

Growth ... Repent

Hear My Plea

In my silence, hear my plea
Take away the "ME" in me.
Help me learn to be like you.
Help me keep my motives true.

Never may I strut and preen
Acting self-importantly
May, instead, I humbly say,
"Lord, I sin. Help me obey!"

Growth ... Repent

My Dirt

 I tracked in the dirt
        And autumn leaves
That stuck to my shoes.
        The carpet gripped
And cleaned off the soles,
        While messing up
The rug and the floor.

I carried the dirt,
        The pain and cares,
The problems of life.
        Gave all to God
Who cleaned off my soul
        And sent me out,
Saying, "Forgiven."

Growth ... Repent

This is My Song

Oh, Lord, this is my song to you.
I vow to be forever true;
To pray, and read Thy Holy word,
And to obey, and follow Thy way.
But Lord, here's my reality,
That in sin, I turn away from Thee.
Oh please hold on!
Don't ever let me go.
Because, Oh Jesus, I do love you so.

Now, Lord, I give my life to you.
Resolve to be forever true.
But then the world intrudes on me.
I fall away; neglect to follow Thee.
Now Lord, please lead me back again.
Enfold me in Your arms so strong.
And then, I'll soar
On eagle's wings this day.
Protect me, Jesus, and help me, or I'll stray.

Growth ... Repent

With

With trembling lips,
In times of stress
And debilitating temptations,
I whisper, "Help me, Lord!"

With teary eyes,
Uncertain of my welcome,
I walked into Your house
And knelt to pray.

With outstretched arms
You comfort and enfold.
With tears of joy,
I whisper, "Thank You, Lord!"

Growth … Repent

By Your Mercies

By Your mercies,
For Your pleasure,
Everything is possible.

Lord, I love You.
Lord, I want to
Open up my heart again.

Please, forgive me.
Help me see how
I destroy my life with sin.

Still my doubts, and
Calm my flutters.
Guide me, Lord, to live for others.

Grant me patience,
Mercy, love,
Until I dwell in Heav'n above.

Growth ... Repent

In the Valley

Lord, I'm traveling through a valley,
        and it feels like death to me.
My way is hot and thirsty ---
        not the way it ought to be!
I am needful of Your mercy
        and I wait here, anxiously,
for the shower of a cloudburst
        of Your blessings down on me.

Do not think I am ungrateful
        of the blessings of the past,
but You said, if I'm in trouble,
        all I had to do was ask.
I am asking, Dear Lord Jesus,
        I am pleading --- on my knees!
Just don't leave me in this valley.
        Let me feel Your healing breeze.

Growth … Repent

Revive My Heart

Revive my heart
Restore my sense of service
Help me fulfill
      My reason for being
      On earth at this time.
Open my vision
      And lay Your will on me.
Unstop my ears
      So I can hear Your call.

Here I am, Lord.
Your servant is listening.

You are not done with me …
      With my growth or with my service
But I am dense, Lord
      So tell me,
           In no uncertain terms,
      What You want of me.

Growth ... Forgiven

The Music of Hell

The music of hell cries out in the dark
The screeches and howls surround me.
They tell of the pain, and suff'ring within,
Of wand'ring souls in torment.

The music of heav'n sings out to the light
The angels surround, protecting.
They sing of Your grace, and infinite care.
Your mercy calms frustrations.

I'm learning to sing Your song in the night.
Your melody sounds within me.
Forgiveness and love flow down from above,
Salvation freely given.

Growth ... Forgiven

Enough

My sin will not hold me
      Deep in despair,
         For Jesus has washed it away.
With grace overflowing,
      Love for my Savior
         Is surely enough for the day.

Growth ... Forgiven

Cleansed

The man at the fair
Took the rings of our promise.
Brushed clean with a cleanser,
Dipped in solution,
Burnished with cloth,
They sparkled with once-grimy vigor.

The God of my life
Took the soul of great promise.
Brushed clean with forgiveness,
Dipped in His blood, and
Burnished with love.
I sparkle with once-grimy vigor.

Growth … Forgiven

Again … and Again

I lie in sin's ravine, Lord … again!
    Helpless, hopeless, worthless, witless.
Remind me of my "before",
    When I knew Your presence,
    When I held my hope in You,
        And both worth and thoughts
        Were as Your child.

Ahhh! Lord, Once again,
Your presence comforts me even now.
    I feel your strength,
    Your calm,
        Your assurance …
And I know that You, O Lord,
    Hold all my ever-afters.

You accompany me in every moment,
You guide my every movement.
You love me, in all that I am,
    And for all I can become.
You await my repentance.

You are the God of my again … and again.

Growth … Changed

Your Sheep

Lord, I need your calming hand
Gripping the wool on my back
To get me in motion again.
Or, with Shepherd's crook,
Gently tug me back.
Bring me Your way, not mine.

Growth … Changed

Maturing

Maturing faith walk,
We're constantly refining
God's work in our lives.

Growth ... Changed

Blessed Are They

Blessed are they who
Walk not, and stand not,
Who sit not with scoffers,
Nor with the ungodly.

If I walk with the scoffer,
I forget my direction.
I wander and waver
Away from the pathway.

Then, I am likely to
Stand as we're talking;
To pause in my journey
Along the right road.

Once standing, I tire,
And sit down with those who
Believe not in God, and
Convince me I'm foolish.

Lord, help me not sit down,
But get up and stand there.
Not standing, I need help
To pick up and get out.

Instead of just walking
Away from the scoffers,
Lord, help me to run back
And into Your arms.

Growth ... Changed

I Was Walking

I was walking with my Savior in the garden through the blooms.
He was telling of His mansion; that's the one with many rooms.
He invited me to live there with the Father from above.
I'm excited! I accepted. I will follow Him in love.

I will follow Christ, my Bridegroom. With the Spirit I will sing.
I will dance, and I will praise Him, as He fits me with His ring.
Ring of substance, ring of promise, ring of hope eternally.
For His blessing and His honor, I submit on bended knee.

I'm convinced that there is nothing, here on earth or Heav'n above,
Nothing that can separate me from my Savior's holy love.
So I'll bow down, and I'll worship, 'til my life on earth is done.
Then I'll go to meet my Savior when my Crown of Life is won.

Growth ... Changed

Mundane

May I ever seek Your presence
In all the mundane details
Of daily life.

Do baby's liquid burps, cat fuzz,
Or what to fix for supper
Really matter?

Baby's giggling joy, kittie's purr,
Pleasure of the family meal,
Enrich my life.

Love Your presence in daily life,
Whatever the circumstance.
I count blessings!

Growth … Changed

That Bump

That bump in my path …
      There to remind me
     To call upon God?
          Did God send it?

That bump in my path …
     Is this obstruction
     A consequence of
         Something done?

That bump in my path …
     Relying on God,
     I'll sing to my Lord
         WHILE facing fears!

Growth ... Changed

Pruned
(John 15:5)

In what way
>> will the branch that is me
be pruned to bear
>> more fruit for Thee?

Growth ... Changed

Strengthen Your Core
(Romans 12:9 TM)

Oh, build up your center
And strengthen your core,
For leaning on Jesus
Will open the door
Of His love.

Love, from the center of who you are,
Don't fake it.
Pretending love and understanding
Won't make it.

Awe and thanksgiving for blessings giv'n,
Present them;.
Sin and temptations? Live for Christ, and
Prevent them.

Learn, then, to listen for Jesus' call
Don't ignore.
Obey in love and serve with your heart.
Spirits soar.

Oh, build up your center
And strengthen your core,
For leaning on Jesus
Will open the door
Of His love.

Growth ... Changed

The Ninety and Nine

Last year
I was the one
He had needed to find.
I'd slipped into a gully
Of my own making.
He rescued me,
And patiently carried me home.

This year
He knows I'm safe
With the ninety and nine.
He goes to find another,
One who was hiding.
We welcomed her,
Encouraging one who'd been blind.

Growth … Changed

Chaff

The chaff holds the kernel,
Protecting from elements
During time of growth.
At winnowing time
        The only value of chaff
            Is its absence.
The grain is pure.

Our sin, dry and husk like,
Destructive and chaotic,
Encloses the mind.
At the end of time,
        The wind of the Spirit
        Destroys the sin,
And we are pure.

Growth … Changed

Use Me

Here am I, use me.
I am not as I should be,
I don't always show the world I am Yours,
But here am I, use me.
I shy away from witnessing.

Do I love you enough?
Never enough …
I fall from Your path,
Yet, here am I, use me.

Lord, I am not the best instrument you could use.
Nevertheless … here am I, use me.
Use me anyway, in any way.

Growth ... Changed

In the Shadow

In the shadow of His wings
I will sing, I will sing.
In the shadow of His wings
I'll sing His praise!

I have learned, in my life,
That whenever troubles loom
I can run to the shelter of His love.
He always welcomes me,
In His presence I am calmed.,
I repent, I'm forgiven, I am loved.

In the birth, life and death,
In His resurrection glow,
I am changed by my Savior, Jesus Christ.
In believing in Him,
I am guided to obey
His call to save in His name.

In the shadow of His wings
I will sing, I will sing.
In the shadow of His wings
I'll sing His praise!

Growth ... Changed

Selah!

How often, O Lord,
Do I pause, or reflect
On Your presence within?
Do I ask for Your guidance?
Would I wait for Your answer?
Would I follow Your leading?

Remind me. O Lord,
To pause, to reflect
On Your purpose for me.
May I hasten to listen,
Then act on Your answer
And accomplish my mission.

Selah!

Growth ... Obey

Because

Because of Your love, I will love.
Because of my love, I'll obey.

I feel You by my side
When troubles come to call.
You guide me through the pains of life,
And hold me, lest I fall.
It wasn't always thus.
For I ignored Your aid.
I waded deeply into sin,
And stumbled on the way.

You came to where I lay,
A filthy, mucked-up life,
Held out Your hand, and pulled me up.
"My child," You said. "My love."
"How could You love," I asked,
"when I've ignored You so?"
You held me close, and smiled at me.
"I died for you, you know."

So now my way is clear,
For You have shown the way.
You taught me how to love You more,
You taught me to obey.
I'm more free than before,
You've brought me to Your light.
When I am puzzled, or confused,
You show what's wrong, what's right.

Because of Your love, I will love.
Because of my love, I'll obey.

Growth ... Obey

Prone to Wallow

I am prone to wallow
In the ditch of the known
Instead of allowing
The pitch of your name.

Lord, help me to listen,
Then help me discern.
When you call me to act,
Then help me obey.

Lord, may I grow
Good fruit for you!
May I ever do thy will.
May I build my house
Upon the Rock
Where winds and rains
      Will never disturb.

Growth ... Obey

Generosity

I give, Lord..
You told me to tithe ---
        And I do.
So, why do others still ask for more?
Yesterday a man asked for help.
        He was homeless
        And hungry.
        Lord, he was dirty!
So, I turned away.

Today I remembered ---
You never turned away
        From one needing help
You paid the Temple tax,
        Yet still fed the hungry
        And healed the leper
        And forgave the sinner.

I have been hungry
        And ill
        And in sin.
You have given me much!
Lord, help me to share
        Beyond the Temple tax.
Help me remember to share of my time
        To share with another.
Don't let me wait to be asked.
        May I perceive their need.

Growth ... Obey

I Choose You

"I choose you," the Master said.
"Only you can work your mission."
I rebelled, then turned away.
I refused to even listen.

"Who will throw?" He calmly asked.
Pebbles dropped as men departed.
"Sin no more," the woman heard.
"Neither will I now condemn you."

"I love you." Then Jesus smiled.
"Willingly I died to save you."
"I choose You," I cry aloud,
"Teach me to obey and serve You!"

Growth ... Obey

If We Refuse

If Joseph refused,
      Said "No" to God's angel,
What would have happened then?
David's line came through Mary,
Who would have wed another.
God's Will be done.
Joseph believed.
      He took Mary, with child.
      Joseph obeyed.

If David refused,
      And stayed with his sheep,
What would have happened then?
Would Goliath defeat the nation,
Or another hero rise?
God's Will be done.
David believed.
      He took stones, no armor;
      God's warrior.

If Moses refused,
      And stopped at the sea,
What would have happened then?
Would Egyptians kill God's people--
Or would Aaron then prevail?
God's Will be done.
Moses believed.
      Red sea parted,
      God's people saved.

If we should refuse,
      Demand our own way,
What would happen then?

The Master keeps calling
'Til someone responds,
Fulfilling God's purpose.
If we believe,
        We'll follow God's way,
        Fulfilling God's plan.

Growth ... Obey

Lord, You Called Me

Lord, You called me. Help me answer. Help me listen to Your call.
When You strum upon my heart strings, let me join Your Heavn'ly choir.
With Your help I'll answer, "Yes, Lord." When You call me, I will stand.
When You beckon, I'll come running, reaching out to grasp Your hand.

Send me forth, Lord, let me serve You. Show me where You want me now.
Those who need me, in what manner? Help me understand Your call.
Let me live the life worth living, Dancing, singing, I will pray.
Ever praising Christ, my Savior, God Who leads from day to day.

God's Attributes ... Creator

In His Hand
(Job 12:10)

The sparrow found its life and form in You --
    Each feather perfect
    Each trill a praise
    To God Almighty.

The baby squirrels play among the leaves --
    They chase each other
    And hide their nuts
    In store for winter.

You hold our life, and every breath we take..
    Your people singing
    We raise our voice
    To praise Your glory.

God's Attributes … Creator

Soul-ful

Gray sky, gray water
Morning mist is blanket thick
My soul is waiting.

God's world is perfect
Sunrise hues on crashing waves
My soul is at peace

Son rises, sun sets
All else insignificant
Trust God, live in faith

White waves pound the shore
Red-gold tree at overlook
My soul sings with God

God's Attributes … Creator

Winter White

Apple trees wear winter-white
Moving with each breeze
The grove, a virtual fairyland,
Proclaiming mystery.

Stately oaks in winter-white
Royal, courtly, tall,
They dance their dance in righteous tune
And show God's mastery.

Evergreens don winter-white
Sway majestically.
They weave, they bow, in pure delight
To hear God's whispering.

Bushes heaped in coat of white
Burdened down with care
They shrug, and wait for God's release.
They praise God's graciousness.

God's Attributes … Creator

I Behold

I behold the leafless tree
Weirdly stretching its ghostlike fingers
  To the heavens.
Overwhelming in majesty
A prayer for His life-giving grace.

I behold the tree in bud
Beginning the springtime renewal
  Of life, of hope
Sparkling with dew in the sunlight
A prayer for renewal of faith.

I behold the leafed-out tree,
Branches whisp'ring as winds flow
  Through the greenery.
Sound calming souls, refreshing minds
A nudge to rejoice in His love.

I behold the autumn tree.
Leaves of red-gold and fuchsia drift down
  To rest on earth.
Outstanding sight of vibrant shades,
They shout of thanksgiving and praise.

God's Attributes ... Creator

Patchwork Quilt

God takes a little of this, and a little of that
        To make His patchwork quilt.

Each life, a square in progress,
        includes:
                Anger's fire-red
                Flash yellow of success
                Disappointment's faded blue
                Dark green of deep content
                Unrelenting black of despair.

God's angels stitch, fitting one to the other
        Changing, as God calls,
        "Wait! Add white of saving grace."

God uses this living patchwork
        To bring comfort to hurting souls
        Who themselves are
        Another square in progress.

God's Attributes ... Creator

You Created My Soul

You created my soul to sing Your song,
You lifted my heart to sing along.
You opened my eyes, that I might see
Your Glory.

You painted my world in vibrant hues;
In reds, and yellows, and greens, and blues.
Then added in birdsong, the chirps and trills
For Glory.

Your children everywhere will need
Your Holy Word, that vital seed.
I'll plant, and You'll water, and they will grow
In Glory.

The Father, the Son, and the Spirit be praised,
My soul to Jesus Christ will be raised.
For when I die, then I will go
To Glory.

Glory, Glory,
Hallelujah story.
My God, the Father, in heaven above
Created me to love.

God's Attributes ... Protector

My Rock

Thou art the Rock on which I stand.
I need not fear ferocious winds.
Thou art the Pillar to which I cling
In my great weakness.
My Rock will never fail me,
No matter how rough the waters.

God's Attributes ... Protector

Shout!
(Psalm 65:7-8 NASB)

You still the roaring
Of the seas,
The tumult of the peoples.
The dawn and sunset
Shout for joy!
What can we do but praise You?

God's Attributes … Protector

The Secret Place

Psalm 31:20 "You hide (me) in the secret place of Your presence…You keep (me) secretly in a shelter…."

In the secret place of Your presence,
Please, hide me, O my Lord!
Keep my presence in Your shelter
A secret from my enemies.

I know I can't hide forever,
But I need some R&R,
A respite from the wars of life.
Hold me, let me breathe awhile.

You've helped in all my battles,
Guarding me from harm.
Now calmed in silence, steeped in mercy,
You urge me go to spread Your love.

God's Attributes ... Protector

Lost or Found

I read in Your Word
      That when one lamb went missing
      You left the flock
      And searched for me.

If ever I need help
      You are there to support me,
      To love and encourage.
      I am safe in Your arms.

But, sometimes faith holds me close.
      You remain there to guide me,
      To chide and correct me.
      I'm still safe with Your love.

Then, I can wait
      With the ninety and nine,
      As You leave the flock
      To search for another.

God's Attributes ... Protector

God of Storms

In the storms of the night,
I know You are there.
In the storms of my life,
You comfort me.
You hold me through
The storms of despair,
And I praise You, Lord,
For You are my GOD!

God's Attributes ... Protector

Psalm on God's Majesty

Lord, my Lord,
> How majestic is Your name!
> How powerful Your might!
> How beautiful it is
>> To call upon You!

You are with me.
You bring me through
> Untold agonies
> Of pain, of doubt.
You are with me.
You bring me through
> Unexpressed joy of
> Rediscovering love, and faith.

With every fiber of my being
I praise You, Lord.
With every heartbeat of my soul
I confess my love.

Lord, my Lord,
> How majestic is Your name!
> How powerful Your might!
> How beautiful it is
>> To call upon You!

God's Attributes ... Comforter

Vacation Spot

I'm not asking to exist
On the mountaintop, O Lord,
Just to visit somewhat higher
Than this valley where I live.
A place where I can rest,
When my soul is so distressed.
A "vacation spot"
Where I can come at will.

I cry out, O Lord, in need
For the comfort of Your arms
There to hide a little longer
From the enemy within.
When I'm feeling most oppressed,
There are times when I request
A "vacation spot"
Where I can come at will.

Lord, whenever will I learn
To depend upon You first,
Then to follow as You lead me?
'twould be simpler if I could.
But when life is mostly messed,
When my life has lost its zest,
Your "vacation spot
Is opened, by Your will.

God's Attributes ... Comforter

The Joy of Rainbows

In the midst of despair is the rainbow
In the midst of sorrow, find joy.

"God never sends more than you can carry."
But Lord, I'm no Mother Theresa!

"Joy comes in the morning."
But what do I do <u>tonight</u>?

"Lo, I am with you always."
Then why do I feel so alone?

"When you call, I will answer."
Speak louder, Lord. I can't hear You.

But, You've shown Your faithfulness over time,
So, in my despair, I will trust.

Help me find the hidden golden nugget
At Your rainbow's end..

God's Attributes … Comforter

My Special Friend

There's a place in my heart reserved for a special friend.
    You more than qualify!
Who else would sit with me when others leave me, broken?
    You need not speak at all.
Who else will dream my dream, will guide my way to victory,
    then dance in joy with me?
Who else knows all my faults, my errors, warts, and failures,
    yet loves me anyway?

In sorrows, pains, and joys
    we walk the road together.

God's Attributes … Comforter

Lord, You Were There

When my loved one lay dying, Lord, You were there.
You were holding one hand, I the other.
She lay between both worlds, uncertain which way.
My hold was an anchor; Yours, freedom to fly.
Joyfully angels did whisper, reluctantly I must let go.
I heard the gasp of pure wonder
As heaven welcomed her home.

God's Attributes ... Comforter

God's Quilt

O Lord, our Comforter,
You bid me come near
      And You will lift me up.
In Your compassion, You abound in love.
You neither accuse, nor harbor Your anger.
      You remove my transgressions.

I lift my eyes to You,
For You, my Maker, will help.
You know my thoughts
      Before I speak.
You gather Your lamb in Your arms
      And carry me close to Your heart.
So I will not be afraid. You uphold me.
      You are my God!
      My soul rests in You alone.

You made my pathway through life's storms.
Your love is not shaken, Your peace remains.
You answer me before I call,
      You hear me, even as I speak.
O Lord, I called; O Lord, You answered.
You rescued me out of my storm.
I rejoice, and put my hope in You.
My spirit was crushed, but You saved me.
My God is my refuge, my strength.
      In my trouble, You came to me.
I praise You, Lord. I trust in You.
      No longer will I fear, for YOU are God!

O Lord, our Comforter,
You bid me near, to lift me up.

God's Attributes ... Comforter

Hush, Hush

"Hush, hush, My child,"
The Father said.
"Be still within
My comforting arms."
Wanting to stay,
I snuggled in.
But Jesus said,
"I need you to go."

"Take strength, My child,
From My loving arms.
Then show My Word
To everyone.
"I'll try," I said,
"If You go with me.
You'll need to push
My spirit along."

"What made you think
I'd send you alone?
My child, I am
A mere prayer away.
Together, we
Can conquer your fears.
Rely on Me,
Your Savior, and Lord."

God's Attributes ... Promise-Keeper

Thou Art the Lord

Thou art the Lord, the Father, the Creator.
Thou art the Lord, the Son, the Christ who saves.
Thou art the Lord, the Holy Spirit, Three-in-One.
And now my song has only just begun.

You love me, Lord, and just to prove Your love for me,
You sent Your Son to earth to die on Calvary.
And I resolve to love Thee, Lord, with all my heart.
Thy people here on earth is where I'll start.

I sing my song. My spirit soars heavenward.
I sing my song, and take Thee at Thy Holy Word.
You've promised me, if I believe, You're my reward,
And I shall be forever with my Lord.

God's Attributes ... Promise-Keeper

Proof?

What proved Your love to Israel?
Red Sea was parted,
Water from a rock,
Manna provided
Enemies destroyed

What proves Your love to me?
Worries departed,
Heart now melted rock,
Comfort provided,
My hatred destroyed.

What proves our love for You?
Self and sin parted,
Faith now solid rock.
Love, once provided,
Cannot be destroyed.

God's Attributes ... Promise-Keeper

A Good Thing

I've got a good thing going.
I call upon You, Lord.
You respond, and calm my fears
Whenever I'm distressed.

I've got a good thing going.
If ever I feel lost
I'll look around to find you
And You will guide me home.

I'll not let go of Jesus,
For You are Lord of all.
You grant me life eternal,
And ever will I praise.

God's Attributes ... Promise-Keeper

Your Song of Peace

You cast out demons
Of fear and of pain,
Granting instead
Your song of peace.

God's Attributes ... Promise-Keeper

God's Silence

When God seems silent
Still should I trust.
He's merely waiting
For me to turn.

When all I can see
Is what I want
How can I visualize
His will for me?

When ears are blocked
By worldly turmoil,
I'm unable to hear
His whispered word.

Drop the scales from my eyes,
Clear the path to my heart.
Once my soul is opened,
I will understand once again.

God's Attributes ... Promise-Keeper

Aging Process

I bemoan the aging process of my body;
The "walking old," the breathing hard,
The wrinkled arms, and pouched-out pot.
Familiar face --
But, sorry, I forgot your name.
Aren't you a friend from former years?

I will praise the aging process of my spirit
Maturing blossoms of my life
Begin to bear a fruitful crop.
Your blessed grace --
In sin forgiv'n, I see Your face.
You are my Friend for all my years.

God's Attributes ... Promise-Keeper

I Do Not Know

I do not know
The time of my demise.
If, when He knocks
    He finds me hip-deep
    In un-repented sin,
        WOE to me!

I do not know
Which gifts He gave to me.
But, when He comes
    And tells me "report,"
    I hope to hear Him say,
        "Well done."

I do not know
If all I do will please
This Lord of Life.
    He says, so I know,
    His grace will love me still.
        Thank GOD!

God's Attributes … Promise-Keeper

How Could I Think?

How could I think You don't know me?
How could I think You don't care?
How could I think You don't see what I do,
When You've knit me together in my mother's womb.

How could I think I don't matter?
You have a plan for my life.
Then, when that life here on earth is o'er,
You invited me to dwell in Your Heav'nly home.

Ev'ry hair on my head You have numbered.
Ev'ry deed that I do is writ down.
Ev'ry blot of my life You've forgiven me
When Your Son died on Calv'ry to redeem my soul.

God's Attributes ... Promise-Keeper

Because of Your Love

Because of Your love, I have hope.
    I am not consumed.
    Great is Your faithfulness!
You tend your sheep from our scattered dangers.
    You proclaim Your Sovereignty!
Though I fell, I rise again.
    Though I sit in darkness, You will light my way.
    You plead my case, and bring me into the light
    Of Your righteousness.
Therefore, I will not worry about tomorrow.

When I ask, seek, knock,
    You give, help me find, and open Your doors.
I will not fear, for You know me,
    And proclaim my worth to You.
When I tire of my burdens,
    You give me rest.

Though troubles come,
    In Christ I have peace,
    For He has overcome the world.
When I believe, then I have life!
You have stilled and quieted my soul.
O God, I will sing every morning,
    For great is Your love and faithfulness!
    Let Your glory shine over all peoples.

Because of Your love,
    I have hope.

God's Attributes … Promise-Keeper

Your Forever Love

I give You thanks for Your goodness,
      I praise Your forever love.
Your uncountable, unfathomed miracles
      Are too numerous to count.
Your plan for me will never be overturned.
Your peace and Your safety calm my sleep.
Listen, O Lord, and hear my prayer.
Your heavens declare Your glory.
You made me trust You from the womb to now.
      You are my God when no one else nears to help.
I fear no evil when You walk with me.
      Surely I will dwell with You forever.

You walk among us as our God.
You show Your greatness;
      By Your mighty deeds You are known.
Yet You are found, in my heart,
      Whenever I look for You.
I know my Lord is my faithful God
      Who keeps the covenant of love to those who love Him.
You put Your word in my heart.
You go before me, and never forsake me.
Beneath me are Your everlasting arms.
Not one of Your promises ever failed!

I give You thanks for Your goodness,
      And praise Your forever love.

God's Attributes ... Forgiver

The Patience of God

It's a good thing *You* have patience, Lord!
Where am I going?
Why am I stumbling?
I find I am losing my cool.

It's a good thing *You* have patience, Lord!
What am I doing?
Who's here to help me?
I'm very confused on this road.

It's a good thing *You* have patience, Lord!
When will I learn that
You're with me always.
I ask for Your guidance and love.

God's Attributes … Forgiver

As Is

Lord, You take me, "As Is."
You accessorize
And devise
The means by which to save me;
To use me.

"As Is" needs cleaning up,
A thorough scrub-down
With mercy.
Sweet forgiveness, freely giv'n,
Cleanses souls.

"As Is" can be "As Was."
Help me sin no more,
To obey
Becomes a heartfelt response
Of my love.

God's Attributes ... Forgiver

Behold
(Rev. 3:20)

Behold,
He stands, knocking,
    Holy sleeves rolled up,
Scrub pail and brushes
    In His hands.
Together, we scrub
    The walls of my heart
    Until they glisten.

God's Attributes … Forgiver

It's Impossible!

Don't tell God, "It's impossible."
    That's when God does His best work:
The Red Sea parted,
Goliath defeated,
Jericho blasted,
Wild lions tamed.

Don't tell God, "It's impossible."
    That's when you're proven wrong:
A lame man walks,
Demons cast out,
Five thousand fed,
Christ raised from dead.

Don't tell God, "It's impossible!"
    Hold on, here come miracles:
Sins are forgiven
Sinners in missions,
You are invited.
Why not say, "Yes"?

God's Attributes ... Forgiver

From the Dark

From the dark of the night to the light of the morning,
From the dark of my sin to the glory of your face,
From the dark of despair to the light of your mercy
That transforms even me with magnificent grace.

Even I, in your love, will be called into your presence.
Even snails persevered and made it to the Ark.
There is hope, because God, through His Son, the Lord, our Savior,
Reaches out to embrace and removes us from dark.

From the dark, from the dark, Lord, you call us to your light.
We repent, you forgive, you remove the guilt of sin.
To you side, to your side, may our journey be unending
Holy Spirit, light your spark so the fires burn within.

God's Attributes … Forgiver

O Love of God

O Love of God, please, melt me down.
Bring my hard heart
      Down to soft, muddy clay.
Refine the lump to purity.
Then mold me again
      As Your child of grace.

God's Attributes ... Forgiver

My Testimony

I wandered
      Into a dark land.
Where terror trembled
      And panic poked.
On my own,
      No comfort
      No solace
      Only grief.

Awakening, I cried out,
      "Lord, forgive!
      "Lord, Help me!"
I heard the cadence
      Of Your voice
      From a far land.

You approached
      Lifted my load,
        Lightened my pathway,
        And led me home.

God's Attributes ... Forgiver

In Your Presence

"From his palace he hears my call; my cry brings me right into his presence -- a private audience." (Psalm 18:6)

O King, in Your palace,
You still hear my call.
Rather than a "long-distance" charge,
I am brought into Your throne room,
Into Your very presence,
And You grant me a private audience!

O King, I am not worthy
To stand in Your presence.
There are times I'd prefer the cost
Of a "long-distance" call
Than to be in Your throne room
Where I am unable to hide deeper thoughts.

O King, Your accessibility
Requires full confession.
No "long-distance" shame, but forgiveness
Freely and lovingly granted. I am awed!
Standing in Your presence,
I resolve to follow Your wishes.

God's Attributes ... Awesome! You are GOD!

Song of Your Presence

My life is finite,
      It will end.
You, Lord, are infinite,
      Extending through eternity.

My life is sinful,
      I turn away.
You, Lord, are faithful,
      Ever merciful and loving.

God's Attributes … Awesome! You are GOD!

Kingdom Eternity

Let every creature
You have made
Rise up in praise,
O Lord.
This generation:
Tell the children
Of all His wondrous works!

For God alone
Contains the pow'r
The majesty,
Of kingdom eternity.

God's Attributes ... Awesome! You are GOD!

Competition?

Regardless of the
      Amount of love
      You've lavished on another,
Enough remains for me.
Your love is infinite ...
      A vast, bottomless pool ...
      Bubbling, outpouring.
You ARE love!

How freeing
      To finally realize
      I've no need to compete
      For Your love!

God's Attributes … Awesome! You are GOD!

Not Competition

It's not a competition
Of who loves more ….
Me? Or You?

You ARE love overflowing!
My love for You
Is my only response.

It's not a competition
Of who loves You more ….
Me? Or another?

You ARE love overflowing!
You proved it with Israel
You've proved it with me!

God's Attributes … Awesome! You are GOD!

The Maze

Life is not a straight line,
Leading directly from birth to death,
In all life's twists,
Blind alleys,
And obstructions.
But a maze, leading to God…
The center is HE
Who, in all purity,
IS,
Himself,
Eternity.

God's Attributes … Awesome! You are GOD!

I, the Lord
(Jeremiah 17: 7, 10)

I, the Lord, will test your heart,
And I will search your mind.
I'll give to you as you deserve …
But, tempered with My grace.

Prove to all that you are Mine,
That you will search My heart
And give to all as you've been giv'n…
Un-stinting in your love.

God's Attributes … Awesome! You are GOD!

In My Deep-Dark

In my deep-dark
In dire pain
One small spark
Of hope remains

Your Spirit fans
That spark alight
By breathing breath
Of holy life.

This promised life
Is not yet mine,
Yet I perceive
Thy love divine!

God's Attributes … Awesome! You are GOD!

Springs
(Ps. 104:10)

He sends forth springs in the valleys of the mountains.
Springs of love in the valleys of disdain
Springs of wisdom in the valleys in decision
Springs of sunshine in the valleys of the rain.

Springs of courage in the valleys of our fearing,
Springs of hope in the valleys of despair,
Springs flow swiftly in the valleys 'tween the mountains
Sprouting blossoms of His glory everywhere.

God's Attributes … Awesome! You are GOD!

Geography of Life

The hills and the valleys of life as we live it
Include schisms of frustrating strife;
Mountains of doubt, indecision, and fear;
And meadows of peace, and delight.
Oasis of calm and the palm trees of green
Refresh us in deserts of doom.
Elsewhere, the snow falls on tips of the battle,
Cooling the heat of our ire.

The merciful love of God's rivers and oceans
Nourish each phase of each life.
Flowing from mountains on into the valleys,
They wash clean, then calm the soul.
Glorious wildflowers bloom on the banks,
In color and odors of joy.
Birds sing their tunes as they flit through the mist
That lies on the mesas of rest.

God's Attributes … Awesome! You are GOD!

Waters of Blessings

Pure waters of blessings
Pour down upon me …
      Clearing my pathway,
      Cleansing my soul.
I see your merciful hand, Lord,
      Bidding me, "Come."
      Bidding me, "Come."

O Lord, my God, You created my world'
Stars, moon, and sunshine, showers and rainbows,
Animals, flowers, friends, and with kinfolk.
Glory abounding! And, all of it "Good!"

Lord, Heavenly Father, I kneel to repent.
Often I fail, and yield to temptation.
Knowing my sin, I beg your forgiveness
Change me, Lord. Bless me, and give me your strength.

O Lord, my God, you have glory and love,
Guidance and power, light to my pathway.
Come with your presence, grant me protection
Come, Holy Spirit, be with me, I pray.

Pure waters of blessings
Pour down upon me …
      Clearing my pathway,
      Cleansing my soul.
I see your merciful hand, Lord,
      Bidding me, "Come."
      Bidding me, "Come."

God's Attributes … Awesome! You are GOD!

You Know Me!

What is it about You, Lord?
What is it about You
    That, as You hold me in Your arms,
    I can gaze into Your eyes,
    And call you "Daddy?"

You know everything about me,
    And yet, You love me still.
In confidence
    I can approach
        Your throne.
Yet, when what I do is evil,
    You still will ease my mind.
I can confess
    To You, and say,
    "I'm wrong!"

What is it about You, Lord?
What is it about You
    That, as You hold me in Your arms,
    I can gaze into Your eyes,
    And call you "Daddy?"

God's Attributes … Awesome! You are GOD!

Why Do You Care?
(Psalm 144: 3-4)

Shadows surround the campfire,
The brief sizzle of dripping juices
       On a smoldering log,
A puff of air that briefly stirs the flame..
We are no more substantial than these.
You, with eternity arround You,
       Care for ---
       More, You LOVE ---
       Each insignificant shadow,
       Each minor sizzle,
       Each breathy puff
            Of your creation.

WHY?
What is it about us, Lord?
Why do You bother?
       Especially when we get our stubborn up?

Yet -- the fact remains:
       You care
       You love
       You bother.
The mystery more than confounds,
       It comforts and completes me.
Therefore, I am capable of caring,
       Of loving,
       Of serving.

God's Attributes … Awesome! You are GOD!

The Hiding Place of Thunder
(Psalm 81, TM)

In the roaring hail of wind
You searched for Me.
In the shaking, quaking earth
You thought to find Me.
In the sudden flash of lightning
You sought to see My face.
      I was not there.

With but a gentle whisper
I called to you.
In the stillness of a thought
I said your name.
From the hiding place of thunder
I spoke and answered you.
      Did you listen?

God's Attributes … Awesome! You are GOD!

Praise!

Praise the Creator,
    The Rock, the Protector,
    The Counselor, Savior,
    The King of all Kings.
Praise Him, all peoples,
    Sing praises, all nations,
    Oh praise Him. Yes, praise Him
    All hearts and all souls!

God, the Creator, designed Him a world
Of puppies and elephants, birdsong, and blossoms.
Man, in rebellion, destroyed all the harmony,
Brought chaos and sin into God's perfect Plan.

God, man's true Rock, has promised redemption.
Currents of chaotic sin pull us downward.
We'll cling to the Rock, still clutching forgiveness,
And rest in the promise of God's holy grace.

God, our Protector, helps, if we but ask Him.
He'll aid as we push away Satan's vast powers.
His Spirit will counsel, and lead us towards Heaven
He grants us His wisdom, then guides us in peace.

Jesus, the Savior, was sent by the Father,
Descended from Heaven to quietly suffer.
He reconciled us, then returned to God's Heaven,
Where now, on His throne, He reigns … King of all kings!

Praise the Creator,
    The Rock, the Protector,
    The Counselor, Savior,
    The King of all Kings.

Praise Him, all peoples,
    Sing praises, all nations,
        Oh praise Him. Yes, praise Him
        All hearts and all souls!

God's Attributes ... Awesome! You are GOD!

Beyond

God's greatness lies beyond discovery.
Love beyond measure
Forgiveness beyond reason
Comfort beyond expectations
Provision beyond need
Encouraging grace,
      Even beyond hope.

Yet God's power lies beyond belief.
To create ... from nothing
To destroy ... returns to nothing
And imagination beyond ... beyond!

God's Attributes ... Awesome! You are GOD!

My Distress

Hear my prayer, O Lord; listen to my cry for mercy.
        Whenever I face trouble, I will call to You.
        My anxieties become Your consolation.
        You bring joy to my soul.
Your way is perfect, Your word is flawless
        Your shield is our refuge.
If you heal me, I am healed,
        If you save me, I am saved.
        You are the One I praise!
You plan to prosper me,
        To give me hope.
        You listen when I come to You.
You refresh my weary soul.
When I ask, You teach me Your mysteries.

See, O Lord, how distressed I am!
        My rebellion brings death to my soul.
But by Your love, You gave Your only Son.
In Jesus Christ, You showed Your glory,
        You walked and lived among us.
        From Your grace, we receive blessings.
His life gives us life to enjoy to the full.
        The Good Shepherd lay down His very life.
Now, with You, He prepares a place for us,
        And He will return to take me home.
He leaves me with His peace -- I will not fear!
Jesus loves me, and chose me
        To bear His lasting fruit.

O Lord, our Comforter,
        I am in distress.
        Bid me near and lift me up.

God's Attributes ... Awesome! You are GOD!

God of My Yesterday

You are the God
    Of all my yesterdays.
You are the God
    Of my right now.
You are the God
    Of all my tomorrows
        On into eternity.
You ARE,
    And
    You are GOD!

Jesus ... His Life

Heroes

The Caped Crusader flew in to save us.
    "POW!" and "KAZAAM!" Situation solved.
    Incarceration insures our safety.

The dog-tagged soldier drove into battle.
    "BLAM!" of bazookas. Freedom ensured.
    The nations at war, depending on US.

The crown of thorns on a cross-hung figure.
    "Father, forgive them." Mercy ensured.
    Bask in His glory. Depend on your God!

Jesus ... His Life

The Visible Image

The visible image
Of invisible God
Is Jesus Christ, our Lord.

Omnipotent Savior,
Everlasting in love,
Has died to set us free.

We worship the Father,
As the Spirit will lead.
And Christ, His only son.

Jesus ... His Life

Joseph, the Forgotten Man

Joseph, the forgotten man--
A loving man, a righteous man
Joseph was a Godly man
Of the Line of David.

Joseph wed a miracle:
The virgin Mary, ripe with Child.
Angels said Immanuel
Would be the Baby Jesus

Joseph went to Bethlehem
He swept the stall, and held her hand.
Gently laid the Baby Boy
In a hay-filled manger.

Joseph combed the sheep that night.
With wool so soft, he wrapped the Child.
Joseph sang a lullaby as
Mary rocked the Baby.

Joseph was a daddy now
For he took Jesus as his own
To fulfill the Prophecy of
Grace through line of David.

We become a child of God,
Adopted into family.
Fully loved, completely saved,
Children of the Father.

Jesus ... His Life

In This Season of Lent

In this season of Lent, please help us remember,
Not only the death of our Lord, Jesus Christ,
But His resurrection, and return to the throne room
To sit at the right hand of God.

I pray, I confess, I repent, O my Lord--
Daily, I sin against You.
Hour by hour? No, moment by moment
I disappoint and offend.

My merciful Lord sacrificed His own Son.
My sin was a nail in His cross.
What was God's purpose for passion and suff'ring?
He wanted His children restored!

In this season of Lent, please help us remember,
Not only the death of our Lord, Jesus Christ,
But His resurrection, and return to the throne room
To speak from the right hand of God.

Jesus ... His Passion

Fragrant Aroma?
(Ephesians 5:1-2)

As Christ first loved you,
Gave Himself up for you,
An offering and sacrifice,
He became to God
A fragrant aroma.
He lived, and He died, in love.

When you promise God
All your service and love,
In offering and sacrifice,
Are you just a smell?
Or a fragrant aroma?
Begrudging, or freely giv'n?

Jesus ... His Passion

Seder

As servant of my Lord,
      May I wash your feet?
I dip the bitter herb of sin
      Into salty tears
      Of regret
      Of shame.
I taste sweet hariseth
      Of fruit
      Of joys
      Of blessings given.
Unleavened bread -
      Your body
      Bread from heaven,
      Manna -
Is dipped in pungent spices
      Of hate
      Of curses
      Of betrayal.
Forgiving wine,
      Your blood,
      Prepares a place for me
      In Heaven -
Home
      Jerusalem,
      Where loved ones abide,
      And wait.

Jesus ... His Passion

Even Judas

Jesus always understood
Golgotha loomed.
In choosing His disciples
He chose Judas.

Judas served his Master well.
He did his best.
Treasurer of this small band,
He stayed concerned.

Mary, breaking jar of nard,
Upset Judas.
Why did Jesus not speak out
Regarding waste?

Jesus washed dirty feet of
Even Judas.
Yet, later that same evening,
Judas betrayed.

We have been asked to love Him
To serve others.
He bid us "come," and "Follow."
Will we betray?

Jesus … His Passion

Jesus, My Son

"Jesus, my child, Please, hand me that mallet."
Joseph then taught him the fine art of carpentry.
In every task, Jesus excelled.
Joseph explained, "Son, Jesus, remember …
You are a carpenter."

His Father reminded,
"Jesus, My Son, You are God!"

"Mother," He said, It's time for my leaving."
Mary wiped tears. "I remember the prophecy,"
Then she replied. "Go, and be blessed."
Mary now added, "Jesus, remember,
"You are God-spoken."

His Father reminded,
"Jesus, My Son, You are God!"

In Gethsemane, disciples all sleeping,
Jesus now grappled with fear and depression.
"Abba, oh, Daddy, Please take this cup!
"Not as I will. Lord Father, remember,
"Thy will be done here."

His Father reminded,
"Jesus, My Son, You are God!"

On Calvary's hill, while soldiers threw dice,
Jesus, in agony, cried, "O My God!
"Why do I hang here, forsaken by Thee?"
Jesus cried out. His mother remembered,
The sword-piercing prophecy.

His Father then said,
"I am well pleased. Welcome HOME!"

Jesus ... His Passion

He Was

Lord, He was
Belittled, insulted,
Mocked and tormented,
Betrayed by His friends.

He obeyed.
Hungry were fed as
Your will had requested;
But, still they despised.

There he hung,
Flogged and abandoned.
He died on that cross, for
Your will had been done.

Lord, I know,
Now and forever
I've life everlasting
In heaven with You.

Jesus ... His Passion

You Could Have

You could have said, "No!
    I don't want this!"
    And walked away.
        You did not.
Instead, you stayed there,
    Throughout the pain.
    To bitter end,
        You hung there.

But then you burst through
    Into glory,
    And rose again.
        Hosannah!

Because of Your love,
    All who believe
    Are given life
        Eternal.
Glorious beginnings
    Are promised us.
    Praise and honor
        We give You!

Jesus ... His Victory

Your World Is Glorious

Lord, Your world is glorious.
Seasons change from bright to shadow.
The springtime daffodils and greening trees,
And summer's blazing sun and cooling rain,
Red maples lining autumn roads and hillside,
Winter's icicles and snow-heaped fields ---
    All are glorious!

Life o'er death victorious.
Jesus rode with loud Hosannas,
Dipped bread in wine to feed His followers.
Good Friday He hung crucified for me.
On Saturday the world in silence waited,
And Sunday Christ arose from stone-closed grave.
    Life victorious!

Jesus Christ reigns over us.
Love and mercy now surround us.
Our sins forgiv'n, however black the stain,
And comfort giv'n in all life's circumstance.
Our God beside us, guiding each decision.
Spirit stirs our hearts to share our love.
    He reigns over us.

        World is glorious,
        Life victorious.
        Jesus Christ reigns over us!

Jesus ... His Victory

Resurrection

Through His suffering to the death,
    We are saved.
Through His rising from the grave,
    We have life.

Through the mercy of the Father,
    We're forgiven.
Through this resurrection glory,
    We've been blessed.

Jesus … His Victory

Easter

'Tis Easter morn,
Our Savior is with us.
He'll silently come when we call on His Name.
So let us worship
Messiah this morning,
Who died on the cross that our life we may gain.

Jesus ... His Victory

Easter Miracle

Easter miracle
Son rises, Son resurrects
Salvation Promise

Jesus ... His Victory

A Question

Jesus as Savior
Loved, suffered, and died for us.
... How will that change me?

Jesus ... His Victory

Road to Emmaus
(Luke 24: 13-35)

Jesus comes on our road to Emmaus
When hearts are fretful, unsure.
He comes, talks, and walks right alongside us,
Asking, "What troubles your soul?"

He serves us His Word, our eyes are then opened.
How to respond to His Presence?
Return to our brothers, tell all the others --
Hasten to shout out our joy.

My Response ... Attitudes

Are You A Pharisee??

Are you a Pharisee
Fervently following
      the law,
Yet frequently forgetting
      to follow the love?

Are you a Pharisee,
Craving recognition in the church,
      Or can you give
Carefully, quietly
      In love?

My Response ... Attitudes

You Are

You are my God, and I will always love You.
You are my God, and ever will I praise.
You are my God, my heartbeat, and my breathing.
You are my God, my food, my drink, my life.
You are my God, Your grace and truth uphold me.
You are my God, and I will follow You.

Oh, Holy God, Your majesty o'erwhelms me.
Most Holy Lord, protect me from all harm.
Oh, Holy God, You guide me and chastise me.
Most Holy Lord, You hold me in Your arms.
Oh, Holy God, we honor and we thank You.
Most Holy Lord, we bless and praise Your name!

My Response ... Attitudes

Just An Opinion?

"You believe," my friend once said,
"And that's OK."
      As though believing
      The very existence of God
      Could be "just an opinion."

God is NOT just an idea,
God is a Living Presence!
God meets with me ... daily.
God's strength and Gods love are mine!
I do NOT just "believe" ....
I Know!

I KNOW!

My Response ... Attitudes

My Attitude

My attitude determines
Whether or not I enjoy life.

In my "gifting," and "calling,"
I serve Him and choose to obey.

Not needing to prove my love
Has freed me to give Him my all.

My joy in serving the Lord
Comforts and enriches my life.

My Response ... Attitudes

Without Gratitude

Without gratitude
There is no joy.
Can there be Christmas
Or an Easter
Without the Christ?

Christmas -- just a date
In December?
A time to live through?
Or -- holy birth?

Easter, just a date
In the springtime?
A time to just live through?
Or -- holy life?

Without gratitude
There is no joy.

My Response ... Attitudes

My Joy

My Joy cannot be organized;
It is a GIFT, from God.

O Lord, engage my heart;
Ignite my joy

My Response ... Attitudes

Destination Disease

"Getting there" brings happiness,
So don't dawdle on your way.
Don't stop, or smell the roses,
Get going! Move! Just get there!
Keep your eyes upon the prize.

What about the glorious
Things that happen every day?
When we fixate on the end
We miss blessings on the path.
We'll still "get there," as God wills.

A "Destination Disease"
Misses purpose, giv'n by Christ.
Misses power to fulfill
Journey's mission, gift of God,
The prize of God's great blessings.

My Response ... Attitudes

How Could They?

James and John asked for seats of honor.
How *could* they? Weren't they listening?
Jesus just finished
      Foretelling betrayal,
      The whipping, the death
      That He would endure!

But wait!
How could I ask for *anything* else?
Wasn't I paying attention?
After betrayal,
      And whipping and death,
      Just for my sins,
      Jesus arose.
Then, sending the Spirit
To dwell right inside me,
He called me His *sister*!
A child of the Lord!

What else IS there to ask for?

My Response ... Attitudes

The Goal

When fearful of the future,
    Check your past.
Whenever you worried
    Christ appeared.
His strength in your weakness
    Carried you.
By depending on Jesus,
    You pleased God.

What flaws in your character
    Conquer joy?
Temptations averted
    Strengthen you.
Past, present, and future
    Don't matter.
Just remember your Jesus…
    He's the Goal!

My Response ... Attitudes

In My Silence

In my silence, Hear my praise,
As my life to Thee I raise.
Breathing out my Sin's disgrace,
Breathing in Your Love and grace.

Every deed in life I do,
Every thought I have of You,
Looking up to You above,
Every heartbeat shouts my love.

My Response ... Attitudes

Be

Be joyful!
I could choose to grumble,
      Allowing the bloom
      To blight my life.
Or ... choose to be joyful.
      Black midnight of pain
      Will cease to rule.
I choose to be joyful!

Be prayerful!
Temptations will gather
      Whenever I stop
      And think of self.
But thinking of others
      Temptations can be
      Triggers to prayers.
I'd rather be prayerful!

Be thankful!
Forget the negatives
      In dealing with life.
      Just look around
I'll deal with positives.
      In each circumstance
      You are with me!
I choose to be thankful!

Be intentional by choice!
      Be joyful
      Be prayerful
      Be thankful
      Be blessed!

My Response ... Attitudes

I Will Not Be Silent

I will not be silent, Lord,
I will lift my voice.
I will praise You, ALL the time.
Let the world rejoice. Rejoice!
Help us make that choice.

We will choose to praise You, Lord,
Though the world intrudes.
Wars, and famine. Pain and suffering.
We have turned away from You,
Yet, You love us still.

Broken vows, and broken dreams,
You've been there before.
The mind erupts, Your calm restores.
When we submit, Your guidance comes ..
As modern as next year.

Why does it take a load of pain
Before we kneel to You?
Your ear attuned to each, You hear ..
Then strengthen, comfort, and assure
With constant grace and love.

I will not be silent, Lord,
I will lift my voice.
I will praise You, ALL the time.
Let the world rejoice. Rejoice!
Help us make that choice.

My Response ... Attitudes

Flowing Love

I am loved
>With a flowing love ...
>One that flows on
>>Into eternity.

Flowing love,
>And the energy,
>Enables me
>>To love and serve my God.

My Response ... Attitudes

My Song

Lord, please accept my song to You.
May my life song bring You joy.
I sing my praise and my devotions,
Honor, love, and obligation.
Actions are my lyrics
As Your tune thrums through my soul.

My Response ... Attitudes

Details

Let Thy power flow through me.
      Use me, Lord.
Direct my steps,
And bring delight
To the details of my life.

Let Thy mercy flow through me,
      Use me, Lord.
Help me forgive,
And show delight
In the details of Your life.

My Response ... Attitudes

From the Bottom

I trust my God
        From the bottom of my heart!
My love will flow
        From the bottom of my soul.
I'll shout Your praise
        At the top of my lungs.
You are my God!
        You're the apex of my life!

My Response ... Attitudes

Heart and Soul

Let my heart flow with compassion,
May my giving be in secret.
Weave Your love into the fabric of my life.

Let my soul be so transparent
That Your light will shine through me.
Weave my life into the pattern of Your love.

My Response ... Attitudes

A Psalm of Gratitude

Hear, O God of all nations,
>Hear as we sing of your glory.
We praise you, O Lord.
>Your river of grace overflows our banks.
In gratitude we sing to you.
>In gratitude we praise you, O Lord.   Selah!

Though all life is not peaceful
>Still we thank you for pockets of peace.
Though anxious thoughts press upon us
>Still we know you are in ultimate control.
Though beset with problems at every turn
>Still we praise you, our Rock, and our Redeemer.

Because of you we live,
>We breathe,
>We have our being.
Because of you our souls rejoice.   Selah!

Blessed are those
>Who acknowledge their dependence
>On the God of all nations.
May our gratitude rise to you
>On the incense of our actions.

My Response ... Attitudes

Funeral Blessings

Though I know that you are grieving,
I'm not sorry to be leaving.
I'm excited, please believe me --
All my sins have been forgiven.
  Daily I will sing His praises.
  Toward the Throne my anthems raise, as
  Angels, with their glowing faces,
  Shout, "Hosannah!" for God's graces.

Do not let my passing bother,
For I'm living with The Father!
Let our lives of love and laughter
Comfort your forever-after.
  Beloved ones, please, don't be frightened --
  Let your trust in God be heightened.
  Jesus says (and I'm delighted)
  Some day we'll be reunited.

My Response ... Actions

I Want to Be

I want to be holy. O, Lord, teach me how
To live for You only. Lord, this is my vow:
To speak with you solely, each day, for an hour,
While others are sleeping. Beginning right now.

For You, the Creator, at home up above,
Made me in Your image, And taught me to love.
I go to my knees, Lord, for You are the King.
I'll worship and bow down. Forever I'll sing.

For You are my Savior, for You are my Lord.
I kneel at Your table, partake of your blood.
Come into my heart, Lord, I'll open the door.
Forgiveness and mercy are mine evermore.

For You, Holy Spirit, bring comfort each day.
You lead me and guide me along life's way.
The path may be rocky, or hilly, or smooth.
Regardless, I'll follow; regardless, I'll love.

O Lord, I will praise You, I'll trust, and obey.
I'll sing of Your glory, I'll serve You each day.
For showers of blessings keep falling on mer.
O Lord, I am singing only for Thee.

My Response ... Actions

Shoulda, Woulda, Coulda

"Help me out," the Master cried.
    "Introduce them to My Bride.
    Tell them that for them I died ..."
        Shoulda, Woulda, Coulda

Once, as Peter, I denied
    That I knew Crist crucified.
    To repent, I truly tried.
        Shoulda, Woulda, Coulda

For my attention, evil vied,
    Then, in my pain, I tried to hide,
    And succumbed to stubborn pride.
        Shoulda, Woulda, Coulda

"Come with Me, stay by My side,
    Live in Heaven, with Me abide,
    All your wants be satisfied ..."
        Shoulda, Woulda, Coulda

Then Jesus, with arms opened wide,
    Called me to that Heavenly ride.
    "Come, My Child, what 'ere betide."
        Shoulda, Woulda, Coulda
    Finally did!

My Response ... Actions

Just Beyond Awareness

Just beyond awareness,
When God "seems" absent,
Old habits begin to rise.
I'd thought them dead ...
    Or at least, in chains.
Once noticed, they return,
    Stronger than before.
And again, I repent.
"Help me," I cry out.
"I cannot resist alone!"

When will I realize
God is never "absent?"
He's always watching over me.
Is it that I had turned
    To see what lay behind?
The turning invites the evil
    To gain my attention
    Once again.

Keeping Jesus always in my view
    Demands a steady focus,
    A "Commitment," if you will.
Therefore, I declare my intent
    To pray daily, and worship weekly,
    To study His Word, and gather friends in the Spirit.
    To serve, to encourage, to give.
Doing this ensures
    My God will never again seem
    Just beyond awareness.

My Response … Actions

Heartbeat

My heartbeat pulses blood
Throughout my veins
    To feed my body.

My actions are heartbeats
Throughout His world,
    Feeding His Body.

My Response ... Actions

It's My Choice

Without You, Lord, I fumble,
But with You, I am calm.

Without You, Lord, I stumble,
But with You, I walk tall.

Without You, Lord, I fail,
But with You, I prevail!

It's my choice.

My Response ... Actions

A Psalm for Fasting

Fill me, Lord.
Fill me with your grace.

Reaching for the food of the earth
Eating the bounty of our toil,
Fills the body.
Searching for food of the Spirit
Feeding the mind with your Word,
Fills the soul.

Many who fast in public, Lord,
Put on long faces of deprivation
While proclaiming loud praises of self.
They do not please you.
Their rewards come
    From the attentions of their associates.

Those who fast in private, Lord,
Fill the mind completely with you
While singing loud praises of your glory.
These please you, Lord,
Their rewards come
    In the blessings from the Father.

Fill me, Lord. Fill me with your grace.

My Response ... Actions

Salt

May the salt of Your Word
Season my speech.
May I respond to each request
As a student of the Gospel,
Acting from the mind of Christ

My Response ... Actions

But, Wait ....

May my words ever praise You, Lord.
Let others hear what I say,
      Then bow down to worship You.
Let my words ever praise you.

But wait---
      Do my actions fit my words, Lord,
        Or is it, "Do as I say, not as I do?"
Let my actions ever praise You.

But wait---
      Do my thoughts form my actions, Lord,
        Or do I often need to squelch selfish ideas?
Let my thoughts ever praise You.

But wait---
      May You live in the deepest,
          Inner essence of my being!
      Lord, form the thoughts
          Which form the actions
          Which match the words
              Of praise to You, my King!

My Response … Actions

God's Prism

Lord,
help me be
a prism,
a many-faceted individual
in Your world.

Then,
when your Son-light shines through,
Let the world see
the grace and glory
of all your vibrant hues.

My Response … Actions

Water From the Rock
(Exodus 17)

May I be rock-solid in You,
May living water pour through me.
May what I say please You,
May whose I am bring others.

My Response ... Actions

Reconciliation

I can only cry out,
"What is your will, O Lord?"
And I am assured
      You hear,
      You understand.
Because of your faithfulness in my past,
      I wait for you.

My soul is troubled, Lord
      My life disrupted.
He who should love unconditionally
      Is angered
      Because I reprimanded him
My Christian brother is angry.
But, his way was a false way, Lord,
      What should I have done?
      He was wrong!
      I could see no other way.   Selah!

What, Lord? What did you say?
Look to the beam in mine own eye?
I had not noticed it, Lord.
      But it does seem to block my view.
      And now I see more clearly.
May my brother agree to sit and talk with me.
Because of your faithfulness and love for me,
      I wait for you, Lord,
      I ask for your help
      As I listen to my brother.
For it is by your glory alone
      That we may see
      Your will for reconciliation.

My Response ... Actions

In Faith, Hope, and Love

In Faith,
I will walk with my God.
    I trust He will lead me
    Beside the still waters
    And into His garden,
    Where I will live
        In His love.

In Hope,
I will know I am saved.
    I trust His forgiveness
    When I have repented
    Of sins I've committed.
    And I will live
        In His love.

In Love,
I'll respond through His people.
    I trust I will please Him
    By feeding the hungry
    And helping the weary.
    Then, they will know
        He IS love!

My Response ... Actions

Thy Light

May Thy light
So shine through me
That reflected glow
Leads others home.

Light my way
Along the path
That Your will requests
I walk upon

I believe
Direction giv'n
For my life on earth
Will lead me home

Help me give
To all who need.
May I now respond
As You've taught me.

My Response … Actions

You Are Who I Need

Jonah, You are who I need.
In your stubbornness I call, through the belly of the whale.
You will go to Ninevah, there to tell the people all.
You are not alone. I am there, in your every prayer.

Moses, You are who I need.
In your insecurities you will let the people know
It is I who lead them forth to the land of Abraham.
You are not alone. I am there, in your every prayer.

Jesus, You are who I need.
In Your holiness on earth, in Your willingness to plead,
Oh My Son, You are My joy, the most perfect sacrifice.
You are not alone. I am there, in your every prayer.

Children, You are who I need.
There are multitudes to heal, there are multitudes to feed,
There are those who do not know of My mercies and my love.
You are not alone. I am there, in your every prayer.

My Response ... Actions

Bearing Your Burdens

I know you are hurting.
Hands clenched, and all shaking in fear.
We'll meet together and I will listen,
       For I care about you.

You're worried and shaken.
Emotions and patience are thrown.
You cannot hold them in your heart now.
       I hold you in prayer.

We'll lift it to Jesus.
He waits to pour blessings on you --
His love and comfort, understanding.
       Abundantly blessed.

May pain please end quickly.
Together we pray to our Lord.
I'll stand beside you, and hold you close.
       Your burdens we'll share.

My Response ... Actions

My Friend, I Hold You

My friend, I hold you close.
        I hear your pain,
        I feel your frustration.
        My heart is torn in two.

The river of your life
        flows over rocks,
        around the obstructions
        of rapids, cliffs, and roots.

Right now it's hard to bear.
        But don't give up.
        The time is yet coming;
        calmed waters, cooling rest.

Your faith is not in vain,
        you will live true,
        through splendor and sorrow.
        I hold you in my heart

My Response ... Actions

Commission

May we, Your congregation,
Be revived by Your Spirit
To seek out the weary and lost.
Send us out to each neighbor
With the Word of redemption --
Salvation and love through Your cross.

O Lord, give us compassion
To give word of Your mercy
To all those in worry and pain
Who are seeking and searching
For the answers to questions
Regarding a Heaven to gain.

Then please, help us remember
It is not for our pleasure
It's not for our own earthly fame.
But it's all for Your glory
That Your wandering children
Would do all for Your holy Name.

My Response ... Actions

Engage the World
(Disc. 12-7-12)[1]

"Engage the world in ways that bring
God's light into the darkness."
Reflect God's love from deep within your soul.
He first loved you, so start with that,
And bring His love to others.
Console their brokenness and help them heal.

"Engage the world in ways that bring
God's grace into their bondage."
Destructive and dehumanizing wounds
Will fester, unless soothed with balm
Of love, and understanding.
God's peace will cauterize, then calm, their hearts.

"Engage the world in ways that bring
God's life" into the dying
Of moral life, and decency, and hope.
Bring forth His Word, His life, His love,
His sacrifice for sinners.
We can confess, return to Him again.

---

[1] Reference refers to daily devotional reading for December 7, 2012 in *Disciples*, published by The Upper Room.

Made in the USA
San Bernardino, CA
22 November 2013